UKULELE Journal

This Journal Belongs to:

_____

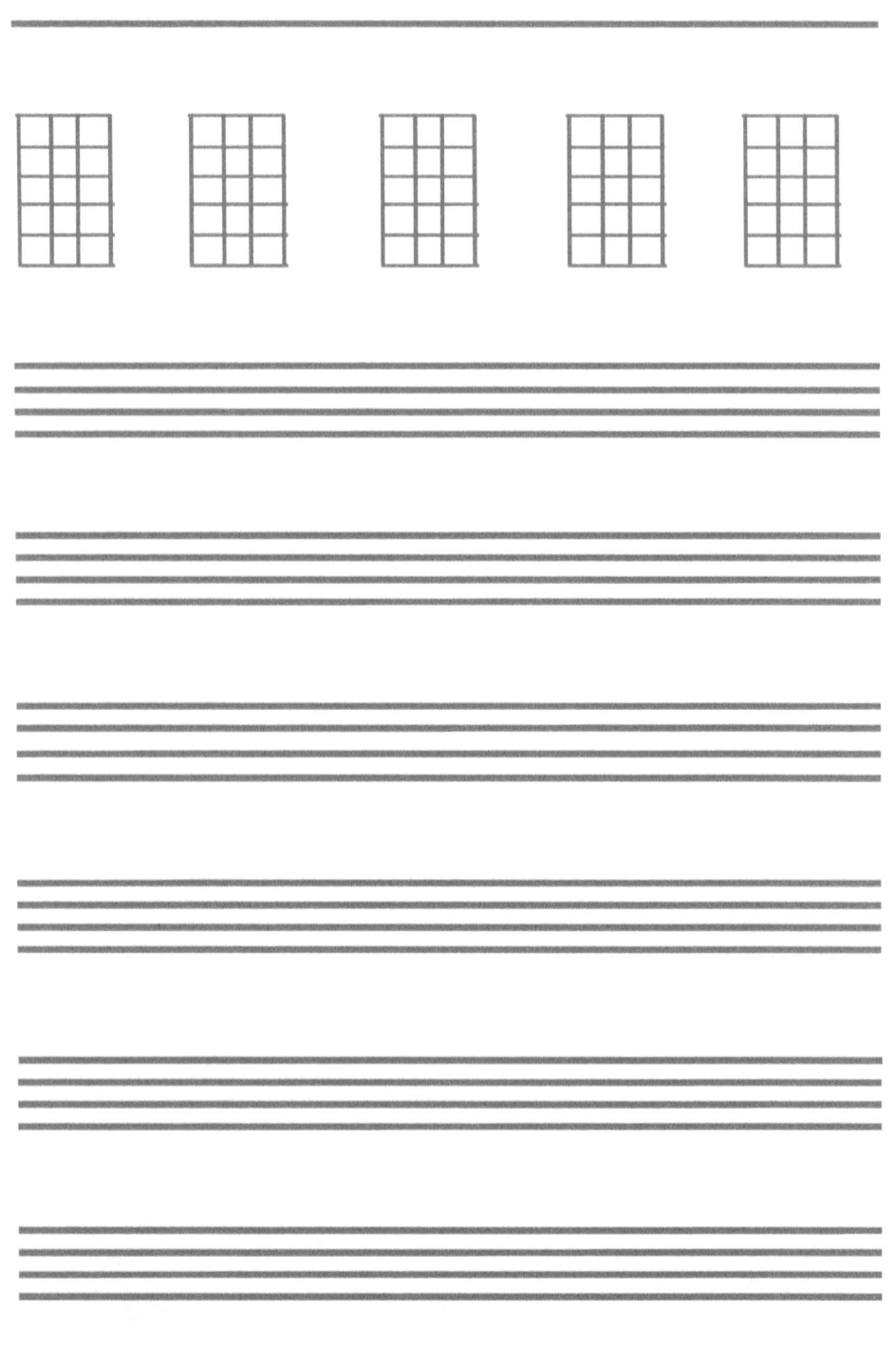

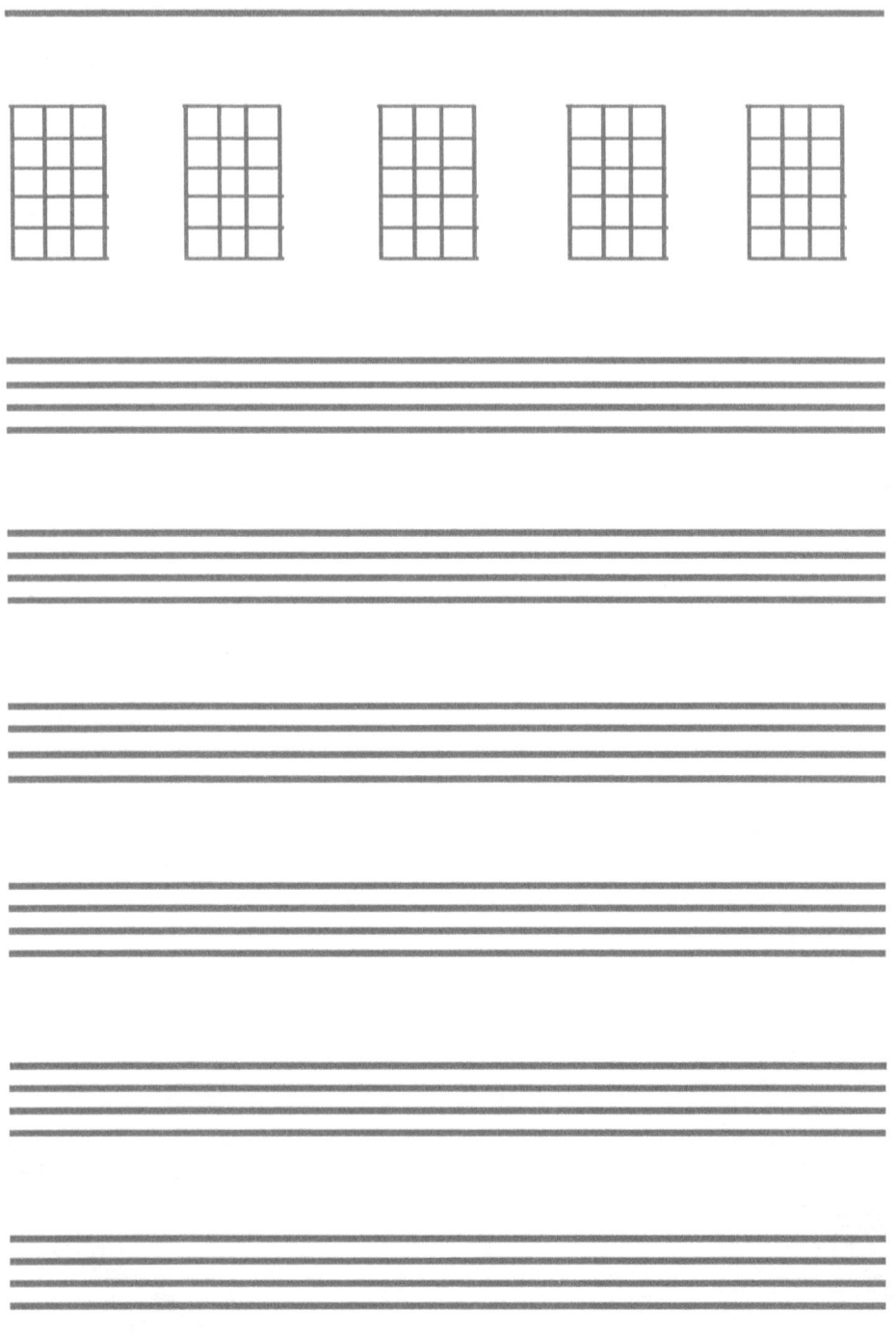

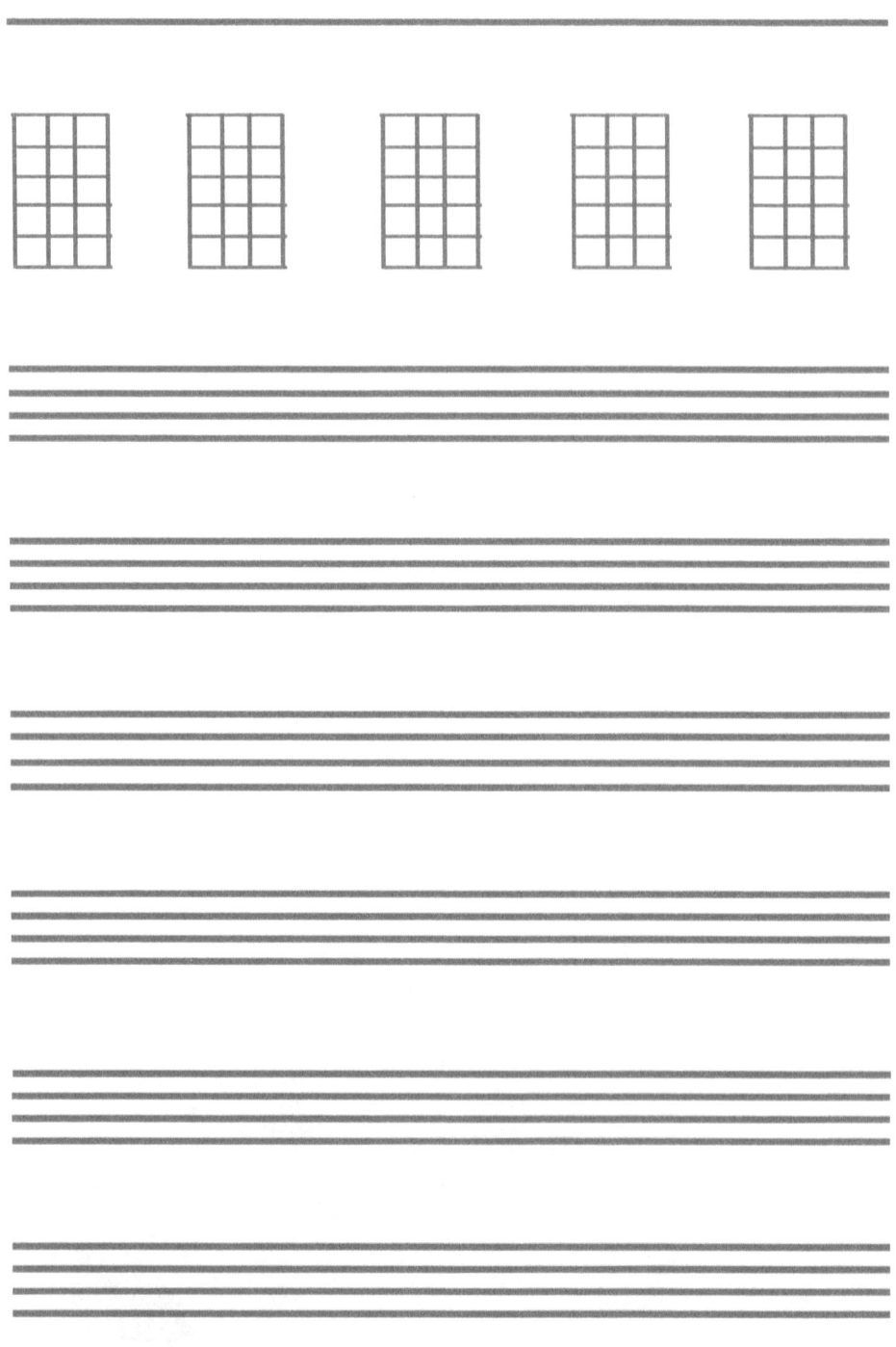

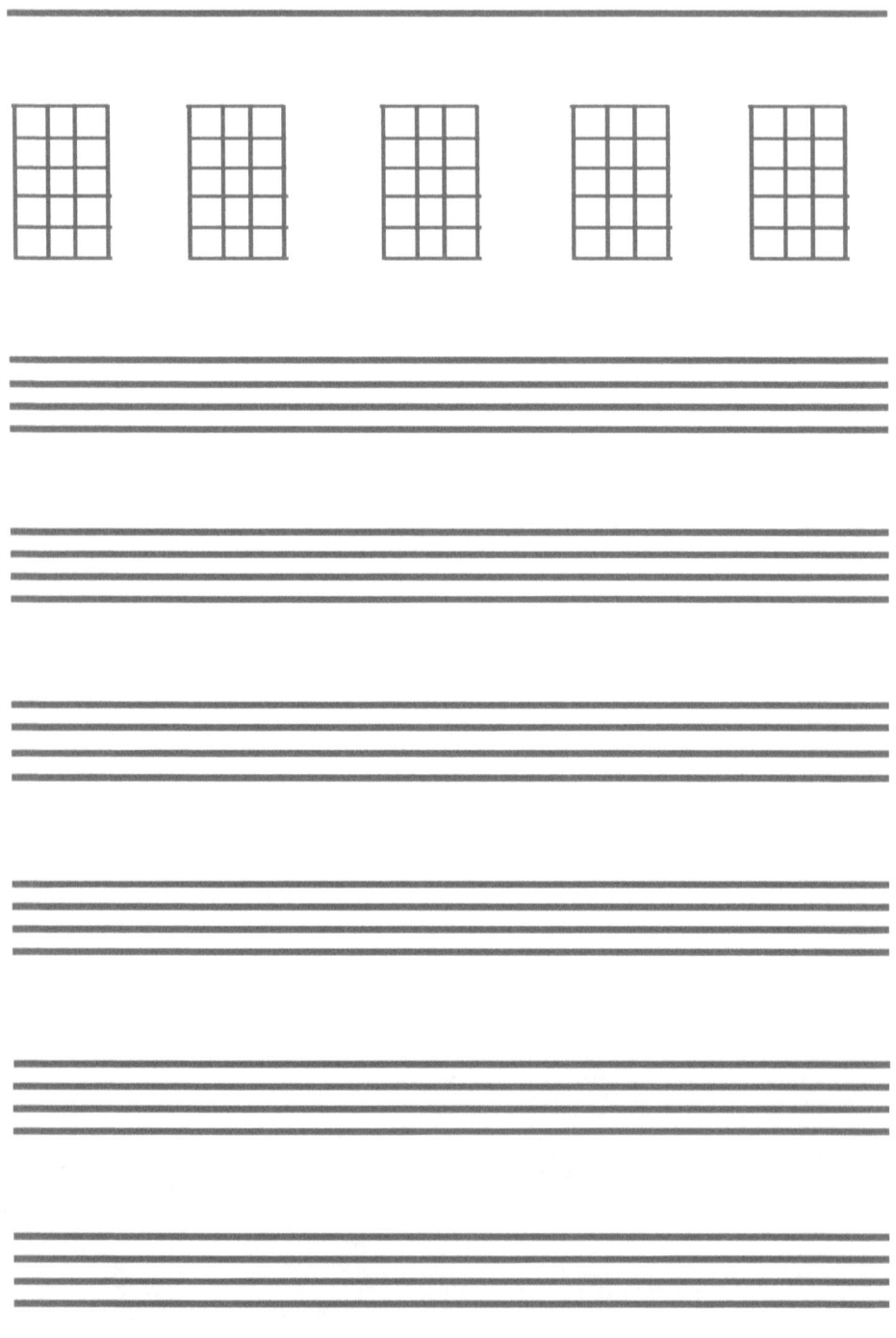

Designed by Kemery C. Oparah

Copyright © 2020 Kemery C. Oparah

The Songwriter's Ukulele Journal (Teal)

Hardcover

ISBN: 978-1-941592-26-7

All rights reserved.
No part of this work may be reproduced, transmitted, or stored in any form or by any means, including but not limited to photocopying, recording, scanning, digitizing, taping, web distribution information networks, or information storage or retrieval systems or any manner whatsoever without prior permission of the author, except where permitted by law.

Books may be purchased in quantity and/or special sales by contacting the publisher, Raise the Bar Learning, L.L.C. at www.raisethebarlearning.com

Printed in the United States of America

10 9 8 7 6 5 4 3 2 1

www.ingramcontent.com/pod-product-compliance
Lightning Source LLC
Chambersburg PA
CBHW020109240426
43661CB00002B/85